Mindfulness
COLOR BY NUMBERS

Mindfulness
COLOR BY NUMBERS

David Woodroffe

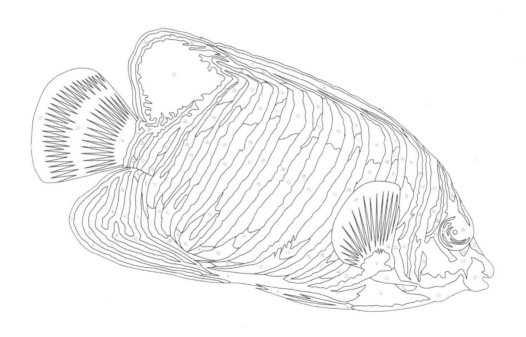

SIRIUS

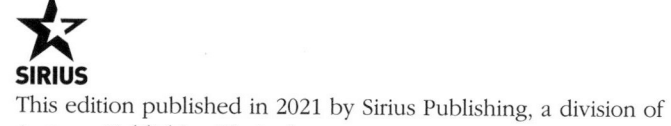

SIRIUS

This edition published in 2021 by Sirius Publishing, a division of
Arcturus Publishing Limited,
26/27 Bickels Yard, 151–153 Bermondsey Street,
London SE1 3HA

ISBN: 978-1-83940-666-9
CH007894NT
Supplier 31, Date 0221, Print run 11318

Printed in the US

Created for children 10+

INTRODUCTION

An activity that allows you to truly concentrate and focus is a great way to make time for yourself, and free your mind of external worries. This varied collection of color-by-number images will provide a great opportunity to slow down for a while through concentrating your energy on a rewarding and creative activity.

The varied images include patterns—both geometric and incorporating natural forms such as flowers and birds—as well as scenes of relaxing sports such as canoeing and surfing, a variety of landscapes, and iconic buildings, such as the Taj Mahal.

The great thing about the compositions in this book is that the work has been done for you—you don't even need to worry about choosing colors. All the images include numbers that correspond to the color key on the back cover flap. Match your pencils or felt-tip pens as closely as possible to the colors in the key—you can even label the pencils with numbers to make things easier. If there is no number, that means the space should be left white or colored with a white pencil.

From the vibrancy of tropical fish, parrots and butterflies to tranquil mountain and countryside scenes, the book will help you to unwind and be mindful while enjoying the great variety of the pictures you are creating.

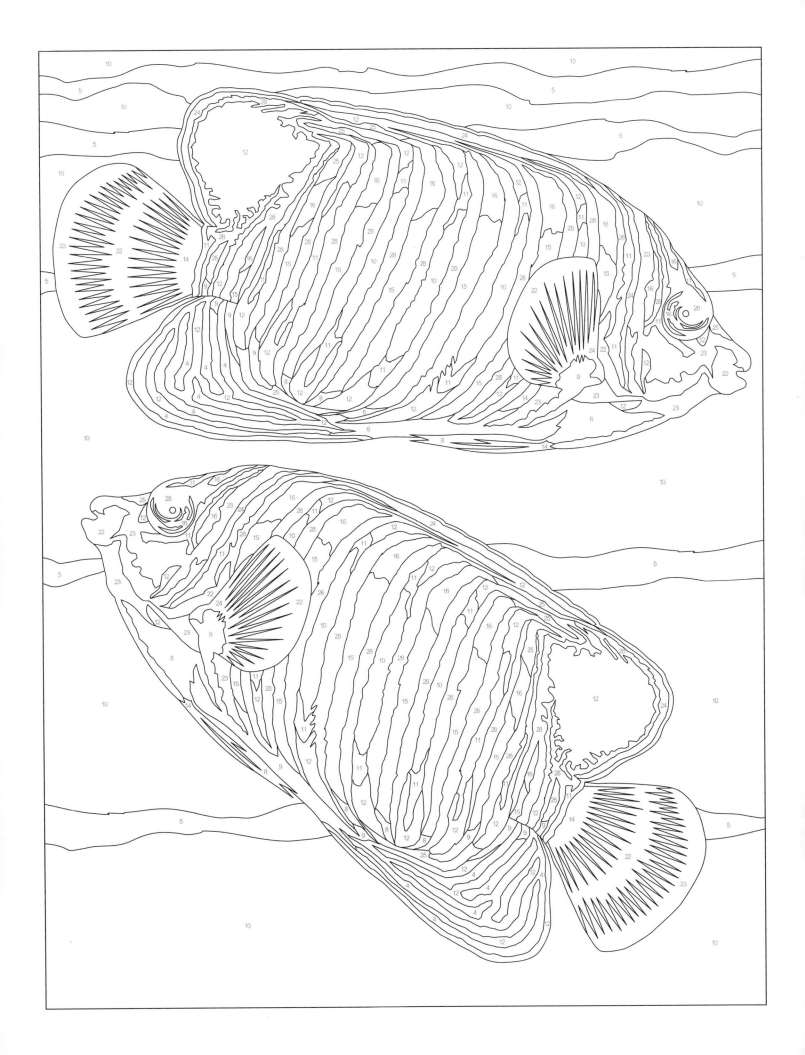

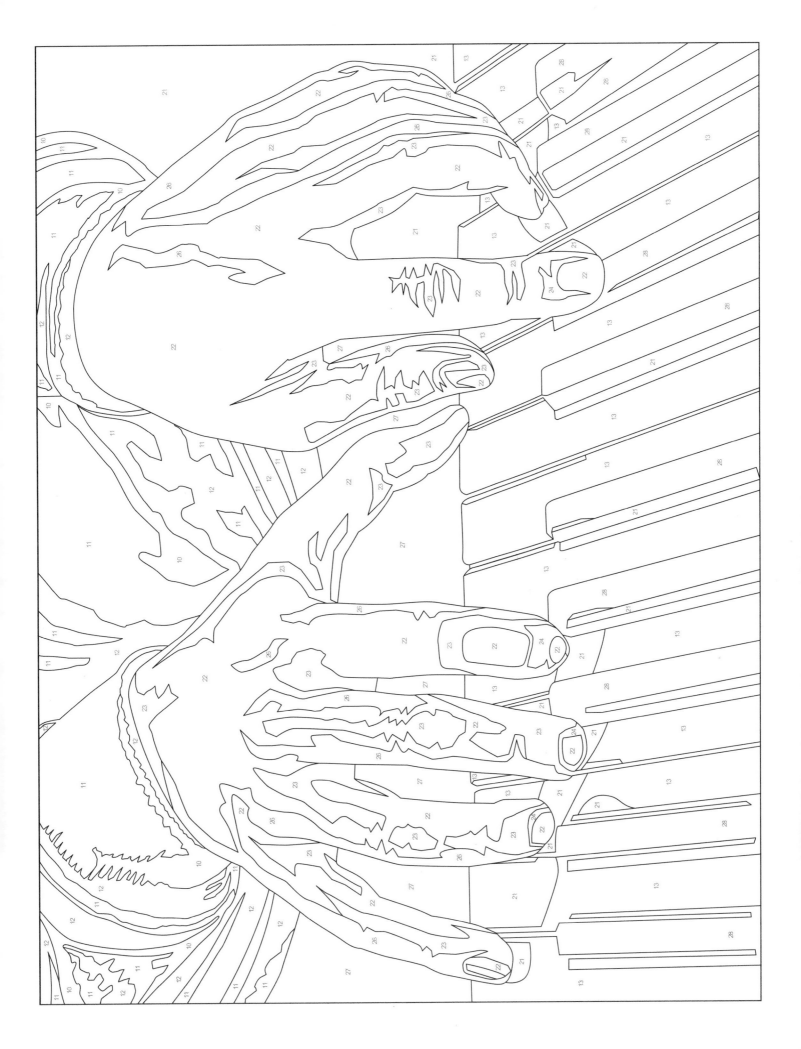

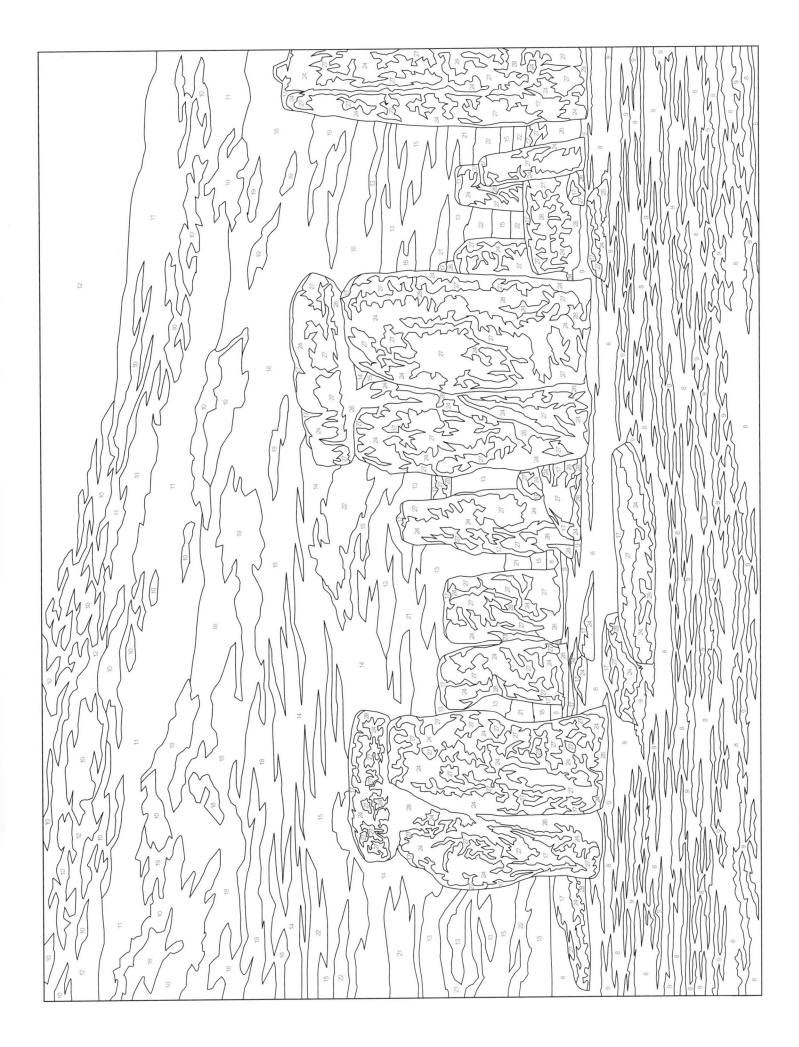

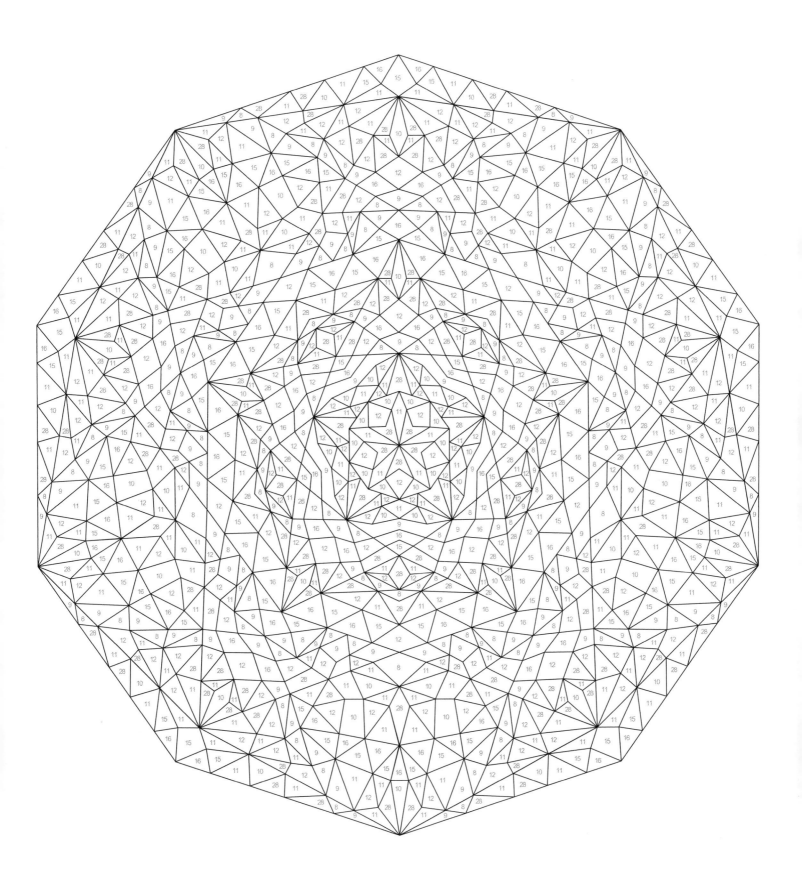

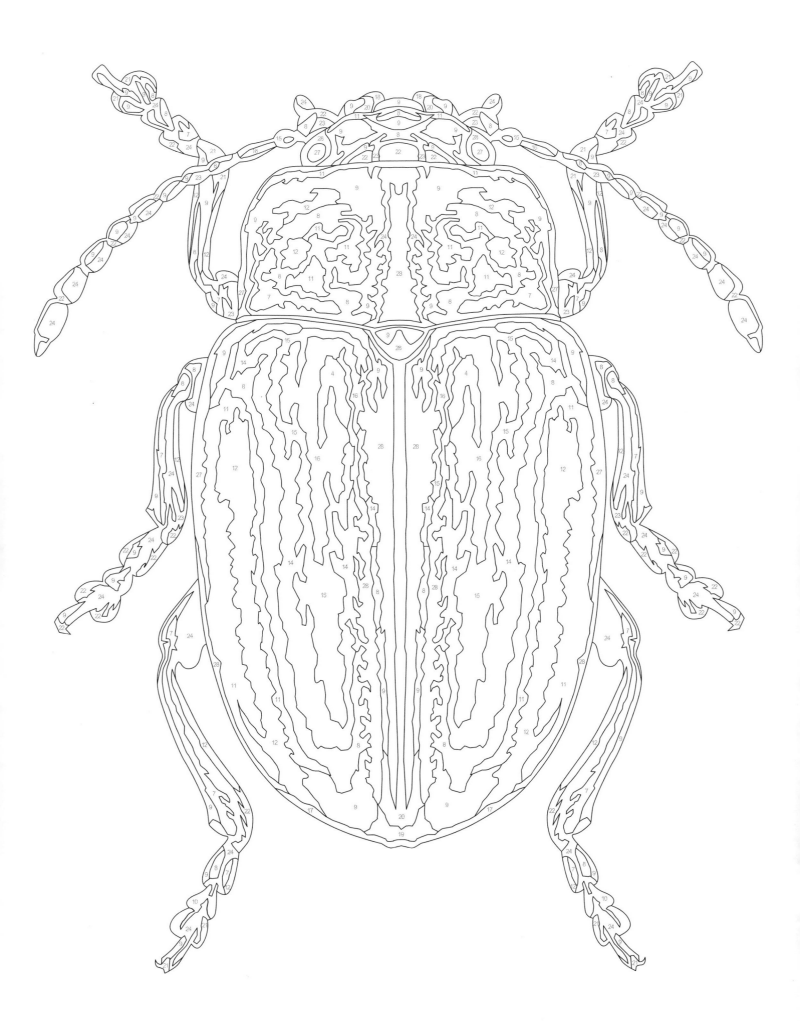

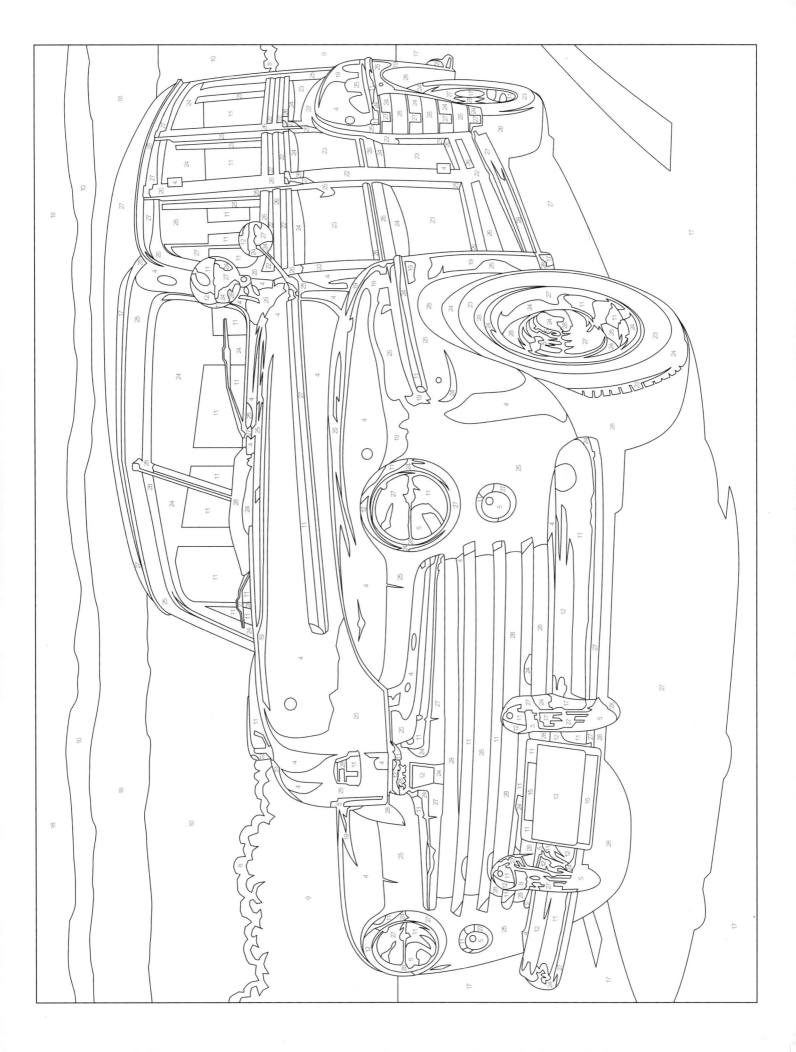

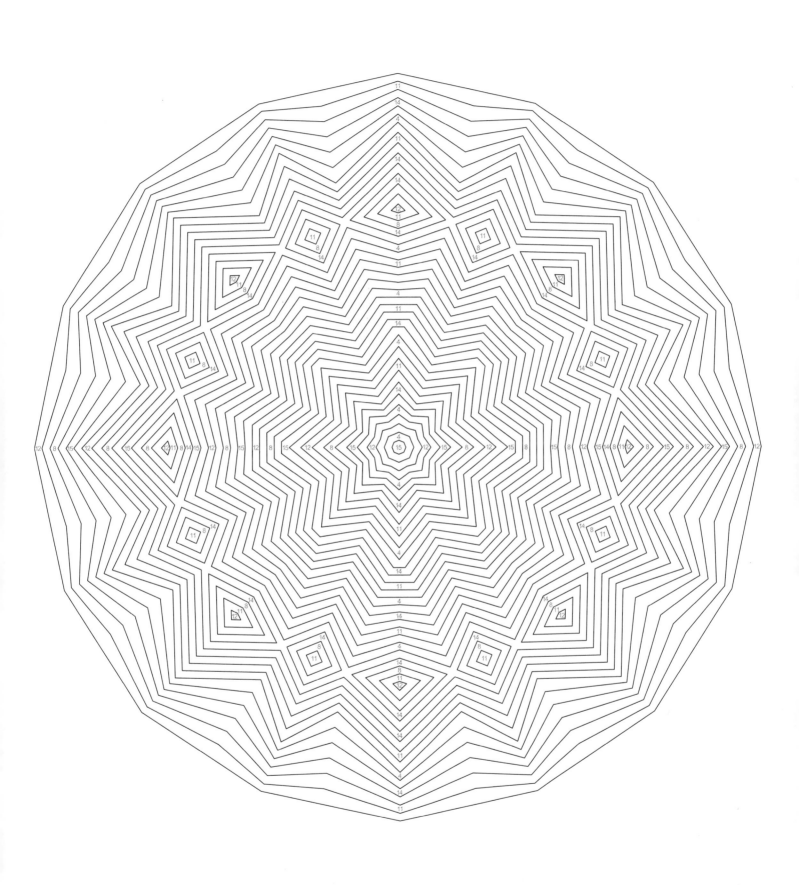